Moreno Valley
Public Library
25480 Alessandro Blvd.
Moreno Valley, CA 92553

April 15, 2013

Jaguars/Jaguares

By Julie Guidone

Reading Consultant: Susan Nations, M.Ed.,
author/literacy coach/consultant in literacy development

Please visit our web site at **www.garethstevens.com**.
For a free catalog describing our list of high-quality books,
call 1-800-542-2595 (USA) or 1-800-387-3178 (Canada).
Our fax: 1-877-542-2596

Library of Congress Cataloging-in-Publication Data

Guidone, Julie.
     (Jaguars. Spanish & English)
     Jaguars / Jaguares / by/por Julie Guidone.
        p. cm. — (Animals that live in the rain forest / Animales de la selva)
     Includes bibliographical references and index.
     ISBN-10: 1-4339-0062-9   ISBN-13: 978-1-4339-0062-4 (lib. bdg.)
     ISBN-10: 1-4339-0112-9   ISBN-13: 978-1-4339-0112-6 (softcover)
     1. Jaguar—Juvenile literature. I. Title. II. Title: Jaguares.
  QL737.C23G8418   2009
  599.75'5—dc22   2008039529

This edition first published in 2009 by
Weekly Reader® Books
An Imprint of Gareth Stevens Publishing
1 Reader's Digest Road
Pleasantville, NY 10570-7000 USA

Executive Managing Editor: Lisa M. Herrington
Senior Editor: Barbara Bakowski
Creative Director: Lisa Donovan
Designers: Michelle Castro, Alexandria Davis
Photo Researcher: Diane Laska-Swanke
Publisher: Keith Garton
Translation: Tatiana Acosta and Guillermo Gutiérrez

Photo Credits: Cover © Shutterstock; pp. 1, 5, 9 (top and inset), 21 © Michael & Patricia Fogden/
Minden Pictures; p. 7 © SA Team/Foto Natura/Minden Pictures; p. 9 (bottom and inset) © Gregory
G. Dimijian/Photo Researchers, Inc.; p. 11 © Photos.com/Jupiterimages Unlimited; pp. 13, 17 © Nick
Gordon/naturepl.com; p. 15 © andy rouse-wildlife/Alamy; p. 19 © Pete Oxford/Minden Pictures

Printed in the United States of America

1 2 3 4 5 6 7 8 9 10 09 08

Table of Contents

– – – – – – – – – – –

Contenido

Boldface words appear in the glossary./
Las palabras en **negrita** aparecen en el glosario.

Big Cats

Jaguars are big cats. They live in **rain forests** in Central and South America. Rain forests are warm, wet woodlands.

- - - - - - - - - - - - - - -

Grandes felinos

Los jaguares son felinos de gran tamaño. Viven en las **selvas tropicales** de América Central y América del Sur. Las selvas tropicales son bosques cálidos y húmedos.

Baby jaguars are called kittens.
A kitten stays with its mother for
one to two years.

- - - - - - - - - - - - - -

Las crías de jaguar se llaman cachorros.
Un cachorro de jaguar vive con su madre
durante uno o dos años.

People sometimes confuse jaguars with leopards. Can you tell the difference? The large spots on the jaguar's fur have smaller spots inside them.

- - - - - - - - - - - - - -

A veces, la gente confunde a los jaguares con los leopardos. ¿Pueden ver en qué se diferencian? La piel del jaguar tiene manchitas dentro de las manchas grandes.

jaguar/
jaguar

leopard/
leopardo

9

Hunting and Swimming

Jaguars eat almost anything they can catch. Sometimes they climb trees to hunt monkeys and sloths.

- - - - - - - - - - - - - -

Cazar y nadar

Los jaguares comen casi cualquier animal que puedan atrapar. A veces, trepan a los árboles para cazar monos y perezosos.

Jaguars often hunt close to rivers.
They pull fish, turtles, and alligators
from the water.

- - - - - - - - - - - - - -

Los jaguares suelen cazar cerca
de ríos. En el agua, atrapan peces,
tortugas y caimanes.

turtle/
tortuga

Jaguars use their strong jaws and sharp teeth to eat **prey**. Prey are animals that are killed for food.

- - - - - - - - - - - - - -

Los jaguares usan sus fuertes mandíbulas y sus afilados dientes para comerse a sus **presas**. Las presas son animales que son cazados y devorados por otros animales.

jaw/
mandíbula

teeth/
dientes

15

Jaguars are strong swimmers.
They bathe, rest, and play in rain
forest streams.

_ _ _ _ _ _ _ _ _ _ _ _ _ _

Los jaguares son buenos nadadores.
Estos animales se bañan, descansan
y juegan en los arroyos de la selva.

Save the Jaguars

Jaguars are **endangered**. They are at risk of dying out. People kill jaguars that try to eat farm animals. People also kill jaguars for their fur.

- - - - - - - - - - - - - - -

Salvemos a los jaguares

Los jaguares están **en peligro de extinción**. Corren el riesgo de desaparecer. Algunas personas matan a los jaguares que tratan de cazar animales de granja. Otras los matan para hacerse con la piel.

Areas of the rain forest have been cleared for farms. Jaguars do not have as much land as they need. People are working to protect the rain forests and the jaguars.

- - - - - - - - - - - - - -

Muchas áreas de la selva tropical han sido despejadas para construir granjas. Los jaguares no tienen suficiente terreno. Algunas personas se esfuerzan por proteger las selvas tropicales y a los jaguares.

Glossary/Glosario

endangered: in danger of dying out completely

prey: animals that are killed for food

rain forests: warm, rainy woodlands with many types of plants and animals

- -

en peligro de extinción: que corre el riesgo de desaparecer

presas: animales que son cazados y devorados por otros animales

selva tropical: bosque cálido y húmedo donde viven muchos tipos de animales y plantas

For More Information/Más información

Books/Libros

Explorando la selva tropical con una científica/
Exploring the Rain Forest with a Scientist. I Like Science!
Bilingual (series). Judith Williams (Enslow Publishers, 2008)

On the Banks of the Amazon/En las orillas del Amazonas.
Nancy Kelly Allen (Raven Tree Press, 2004)

Web Sites/Páginas web

Defenders of Wildlife: Jaguar/Defensores de la fauna: El jaguar
www.defenders.org/wildlife_and_habitat/wildlife/jaguar.php
Read facts about jaguars. You can even listen to a jaguar roar!/
Lean datos sobre los jaguares. ¡Hasta pueden oír rugir
a un jaguar!

**Enchanted Learning: All About Rain Forests/
Las selvas tropicales**
www.enchantedlearning.com/subjects/rainforest
Learn more about rain forests and the animals that live there./
Conozcan mejor las selvas tropicales y a los animales
que las habitan.

Index/Índice

About the Author

Julie Guidone has taught kindergarten and first and second grades in Madison, Connecticut, and Fayetteville, New York. She loves to take her students on field trips to the zoo to learn about all kinds of animals! She lives in Syracuse, New York, with her husband, Chris, and her son, Anthony.

- - - - - - - - - - - - - -

Información sobre la autora

Julie Guidone ha sido maestra de jardín de infancia, y de primero y segundo grado en Madison, Connecticut, y en Fayetteville, Nueva York. ¡A Julie le encanta ir de excursión al zoológico con sus alumnos para que conozcan todo tipo de animales! Julie vive en Syracuse, Nueva York, con su esposo Chris y su hijo Anthony.